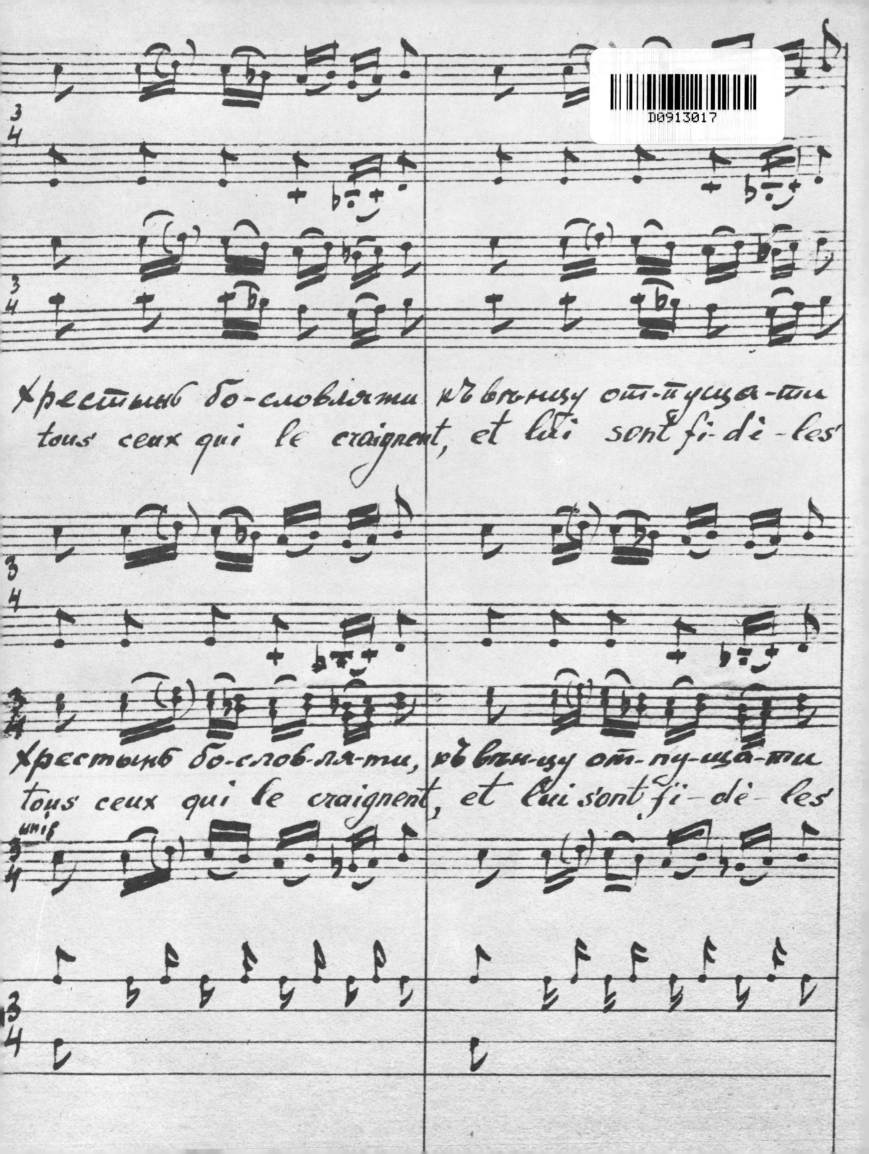

Хрестьнь бо-словляти къ вьницу от-пуща-ти
tous ceux qui le craignent, et lui sont fi-dè-les

Хрестынъ бо-слов-ля-ти, къ вьницу от-пу-ща-ти
tous ceux qui le craignent, et lui sont fi-dè-les

time," "time stands still," "time marches on," and the rest. And similarly with "all your life": "*so much* life" is its Stravinskian sense.

So much life, and so much time, are concentrated in this delightful and formidable Stravinsky. Sitting in the Hollywood house where he now lives, you are, as Robert Craft points out, only a few hundred yards from the grotesqueries of the Sunset Strip; but the banal sensationalism down the road is colorless compared with the excitement that assails you if you are of the historically impressionable type and find yourself reflecting—as a start—that your host was Rimsky-Korsakov's pupil. That in 1908 he composed in memory of Rimsky-Korsakov a *Funeral Dirge* whose score was lost during the Russian Revolution, and now in 1967 has had a recording of the new *Requiem Canticles* played at a Princeton service in memory of his friend Robert Oppenheimer; that he was Diaghilev's "discovery" ("Take a good look at him: he's a man about to be famous!"), greatly admired by Debussy and Satie, and yet today, as Robert Craft puts it, younger people are just learning to be his contemporaries. Many of his works are still to become familiar to the general public—his *Mavra,* for example, or his *Symphony in C.* In other words, his music still holds mysteries and reserves, is still "ahead of its time," in fact beyond time. Cocteau was his librettist in 1925 and Auden in 1948, Picasso his portraitist in 1917 and Giacometti in 1957.

In the charming white-and-green living room of the house in Hollywood, or around the dinner table, reminiscence is far from being the chief climate, though it comes forth richly if requested. "Nijinsky was a weak man—as weak as his muscles were strong"; "Yes, of course Nijinsky made love just to the nymph's scarf: what more would Diaghilev have allowed?"; "Cocteau's first libretto for *Oedipus Rex* was full of ideas. The second was still full of ideas. I told him 'I want not ideas. I want words!'" But soon you find that your host is drawing *you* out, asking you this, asking you that, listening. You remember how firm his grip of welcome was. And you remark the warm, enchanted smile he has when something interests him. Such a diversity of things do interest him, to an extent that is rarely true even of the greatest men. Pushkin and Shakespeare, the presumed euphoria of the ladybug sighted in a nearby bowl of white stock, the nostalgic properties of flower scents, the vanished phenomenon of Hollywood's intellectual colony, almost all things Russian, and every aspect of artistic labor. "When I read Pushkin," he says, "I ask myself not so much 'What is it?' as 'How is it done?' Myself, I am a maker."

When he develops his own penetrating, often astringent, trains of thought he smiles as if being entertained, gleeful as a child at these surprises that are unfolding from his own reasoning. He leans forward in his seat, resting his chin on hands that are clasped over the crook of his black cane, his eyes beaming as he makes his points, as he exercises his intellect. He looks right in your eye, delighting in your interest in him, in his interest in you, in the pleasures of human communion. Here is someone who has kept his wits—not to mention his wit—about him, in the truest sense and to the great good fortune of us all.

—Francis Steegmuller

STRAVINSKY'S VISIT — M. Igor Stravinsky (left), the composer, greeted at Croydon on his arrival from Paris by M. Diaghileff, of the Russian Ballet, to which he has contributed a large share of the music.

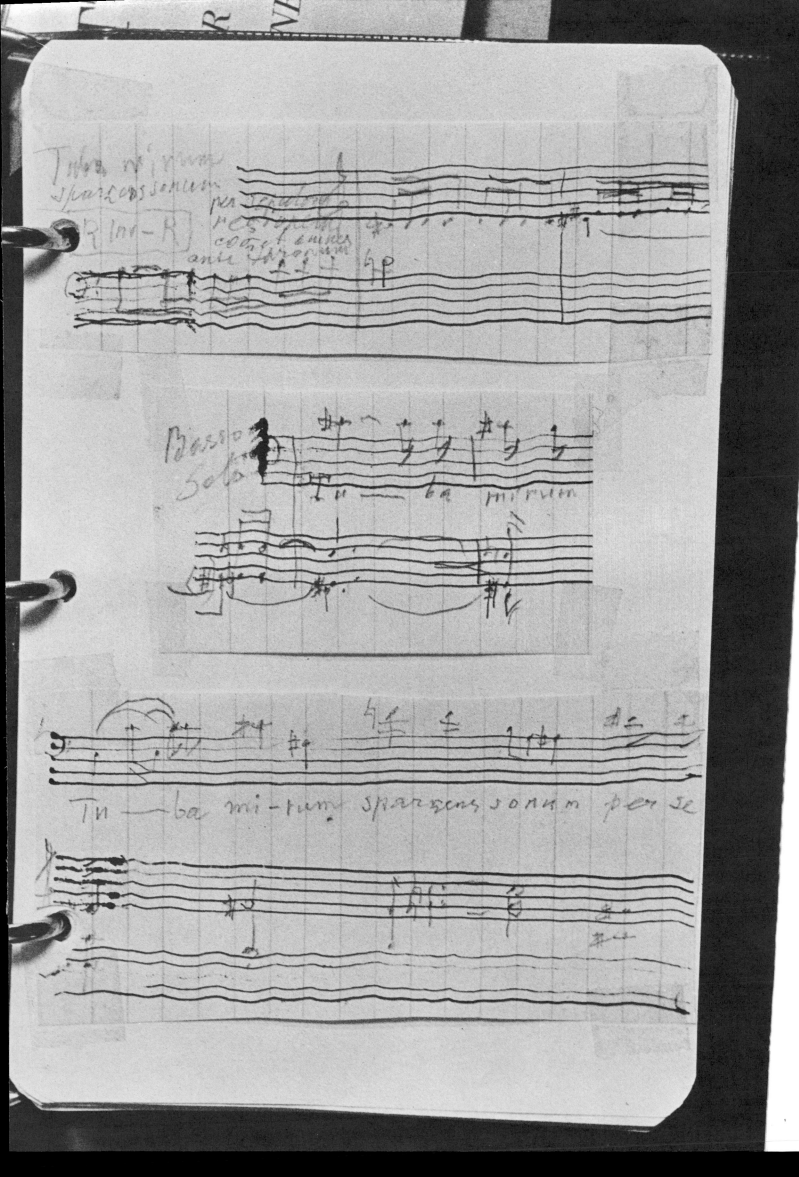

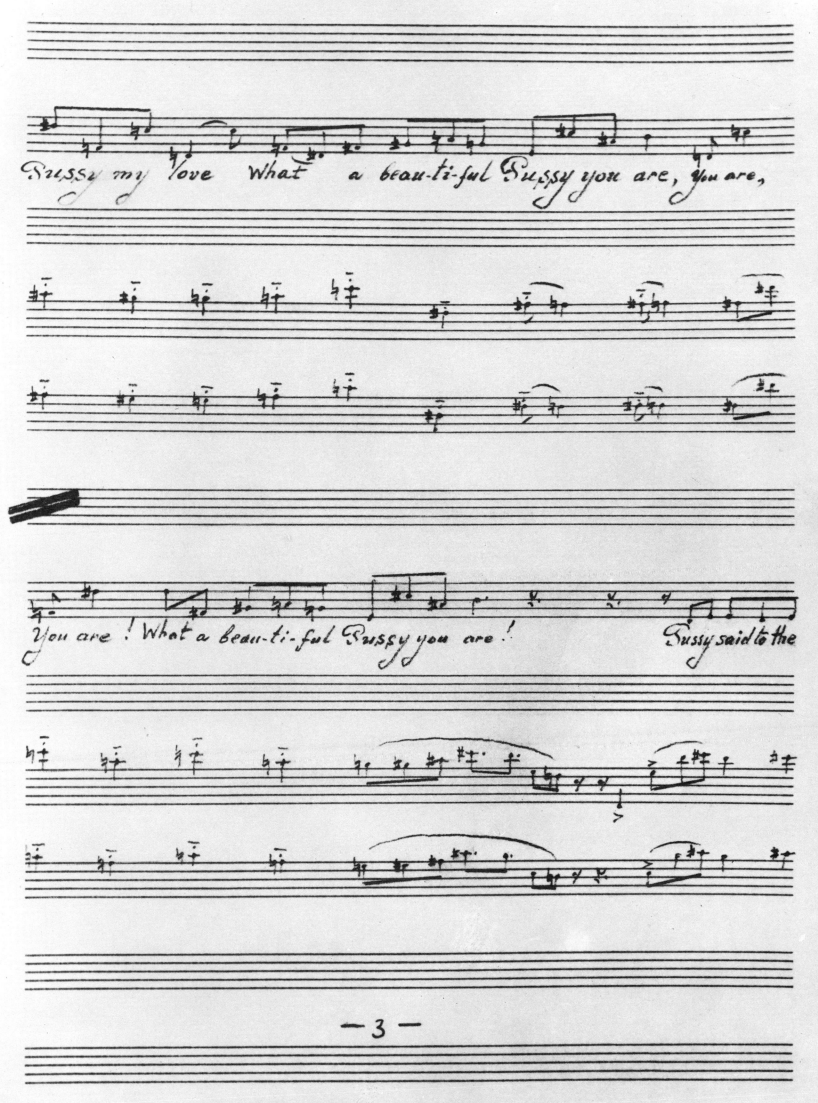

Pussy my love What a beau-ti-ful Pussy you are, you are,

You are! What a beau-ti-ful Pussy you are! Pussy said to the

They sailed a-way, for a year and a day, to the land where the

Bong-tree grows; And there in the wood a Piggy-wig stood,

In his greenroom the composer studied the score of the *Symphonies of Wind Instruments* and, with the thoroughness of a bank robber, planned the post-concert getaway. During intermission he received Dr. Robert Oppenheimer, who had led the standing ovation at the beginning of the concert (and who defied an injunction in the program not to applaud at the end of the *Requiem*); only four months later a recording of the music was played at another gathering in Princeton in Dr. Oppenheimer's memory. The composer is assisted to the stage entrance by orchestra manager Harvey Phillips and Professor Babbitt (who whiled away *his* pre-curtain time breezing through a volume of *IBM Systems Analysis*). Mr. Newman's view of Stravinsky bowing after the performance of his *Mass* is from behind the moppets (soprano section) of the Ithaca College Choir.

A meeting of two veterans, now almost sole survivors of a revolution in art and anti-art; two who challenged and changed the values they were born to, for it is difficult to remember now that they both occupied lonely out- posts once, and that some of the currency of our whole world was at one time theirs alone. Stravinsky and Marcel Duchamp had not seen each other since about 1920. When they parted, Duchamp said, "Well, maestro, see you in another fifty years."

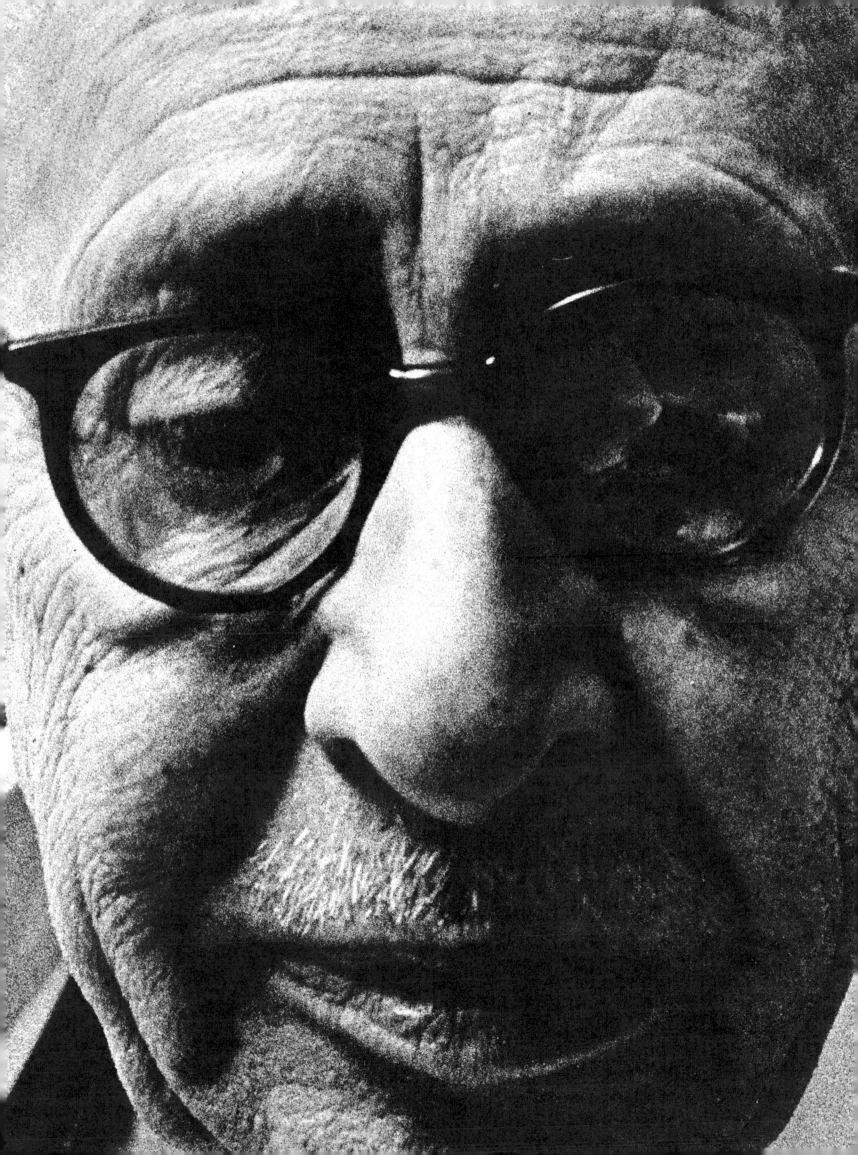

was possible to record this note-by-note sequence of the composer actually composing, only because he had forgotten that Mr. Newman was already in the room photographing still lifes; Stravinsky says he was so absorbed with the music he did not hear the camera. Stravinsky's secondary work, performing his music, was also relatively light during the three months. Concerts were few and light in repertory, and he did not record at all. Nor was his social calendar heavily inscribed, though, as always, the uninvited visitors outnumbered the invited, Stravinsky being a tourist attraction even in the city of movie stars and Disneyland. The largest part of his leisure was claimed by books. He reads continually, with the range of a polymath and the speed of a reviewer, and claims that old age is the best time in life to be a student.

Happily, and rarely true for a period as long as three months, the composer succumbed to no illnesses (apart from hangovers). On the contrary, there was an auspicious improvement in his health. He suffers from a blood disease (polycethemia) that led to cerebral thromboses in 1956 and 1959, the first causing a temporary loss of speech ("a short circuit in the Convolution of Broca," as he describes it), the second partially paralyzing, and leaving permanent claudication in, the right leg. At the end of August (1966), the disease switched course and failed to respond to its (Dracula-like) containing treatment. Roentgen rays were prescribed on the composer's arrival in New York, following a concert in Louisville, September 17, and he was subjected to their action during the week of rehearsals for the Princeton concert as well as in the week following. The reader might reflect that a threat of leukemia hangs over Stravinsky's head, and that he was fully aware of it, during the entire series of New York and Princeton photographs. Fortunately, the effects of the radiation exceeded all expectations, as the composer learned after returning home, where within two weeks analysis showed a perfect restoration of all chemical percentages and balances.

The chronicle of outer events during the three months included brief treks, for pairs of concerts, to Honolulu (mid-November), Portland (the beginning of December), and Chicago (the end of December). Portland was less exotic than Honolulu, in spite of perpetual rain and, at the Hilton, mentholated toothpicks and Japanese waitresses (very pretty as they lined up to sing "Happy Bird-Day To oo" for one of our guests; and intelligent as well, having quickly learned to ask Mr. Stravinsky, "You wish care more Scots whisky pease?"). But the Oregon concerts were satisfying (what a wealth of good underpaid musicians there is in America!), and Governor Hatfield himself came backstage to greet Mr. Stravinsky, later sending a medal, a fact I remark because our Presidential hopefuls are usually more careful to keep their distance from the arts, at least in public.

The Stravinskys arrived in Chicago at the winter solstice and under a goose-flesh sky (in contrast to the pavonian colors and rich sea changes of the Hawaii they had so recently departed). The waves of Lake Michigan appeared to have turned to ice at their crests, and the surf to have frozen in midspray, but the Stravinskys, answering the call of their septentrional childhoods, went out into the snow to—that is what they would have done, anyway—play. The composer received ovations from the Chicago audiences, the tusch from the orchestra, and the usual reviews from, as he says, deathwatch-beetle reviewers. ("Stravinsky is the greatest living composer, and I say that sincerely," wrote one of them, to whom sincerity appears to be exceptional.) Between-times he saw a play, read two volumes of French history and hourly newspaper coverage on Casals' ninetieth birthday ("The master inhaled the morning air, exhaled it, again inhaled, then gazed into the face of Vice-President Humphrey—tear-stained by now and beginning to smear its make-up—declaring, 'I am for humanity.' "). Still another kind of recognition came in the airport on the way to New York, when a teen-age boy, passing us, turned to shout to a companion: "Hey, man, the cat in the wheelchair is IGOR STRAVINSKY!"

"...when we read the poetry of *King Lear* what is it to us how the poet lived?...Peeping and prying into greenroom gossip of the day, the poet's drinking, the poet's debts. We have *King Lear:* and it is immortal." Thus George Russell in *Ulysses.* But Stephen Dedalus' answer, that Shakespeare *is* Hamlet, constitutes the more modern argument. "As we...weave and unweave our bodies...from day to day, their molecules shuttled to and fro, so does the artist weave and unweave his image...so through the ghost of the unquiet father the image of the unliving son looks forth."

Whatever our own views, privacy—which is more and more difficult to define in the modern state as there is less and less of it—is already and no doubt permanently invaded. We are all "on camera," and closed-circuit television, radio-wave detection systems, infrared photography, wiretapping and the other ever-improving "bugging" devices are not likely to restore the castle to the home.

Mr. Newman's *"Histoires Naturelles"* take the viewer into the home, but do not, I think, invade it. Are his pictures true? Is the cameraman more closely bound by fact than the writer, or are their illusionist tricks simply too different to be compared? The answer is that word descriptions can say both more and less than photographs and are therefore not in the same senses either true or untrue; but at least none of Mr. Newman's photographs was posed; there are no pin-ups in the book, certainly, and, to my nose, no whiff of the incense that naturally clouds around the composer. Neither was any situation staged or conjunction of people arranged: Mr. Newman's camera was never coercive. Once, at the beginning of term he exhorted the "maestro" to repeat an action, but the maestro did not comply and was never again prompted. He went about his routine (some routine!) apparently oblivious of the lenses, though whether he really was oblivious except in the composing sequence is difficult to say. One night in a restaurant he called for pen and paper and drew the muzzle-end view of a camera. It looked ominous. (Newman Collection, No. 7693: I.S.)

Like descriptions in a diary, each of these photographs frames and inevitably dramatizes a moment; to the exclusion of other moments, the reader may object, adding that selection distorts by grouping the fragments of a large picture to form a different, smaller picture satisfying another purpose, and providing, at best, a misleading view of the whole that is life itself. Yet memory acts in the same way, and so does art. Mr. Newman has memorized a Stravinsky for all of us, and all who have known the man must agree that each of these recollections is characteristic of one of his many characters.

—Robert Craft